SONGS
FOR THE
FLANNEL BOARD

By Connie Walters

Illustrations by Diane Woods Totten

Publishers
T.S. Denison and Co., Inc.
Minneapolis, Minnesota

Dedication
The author and the illustrator of this book wish to thank their husbands and their children for their encouragement and support.

Standard Book Number: 513-01946-4 Songs For The Flannel Board
Copyright © 1989 by T.S.Denison & Co., Inc.
Minneapolis, Minnesota 55431

INTRODUCTION

Music is one of the best means a teacher has to enhance all areas of growth in child development: emotional, social, physical and intellectual. Singing is fun. Children enjoy the melody, the rhythm and the rhyme of words. They will repeat songs over and over again. Singing is such a pleasureable way for them to learn. Some of the many benefits derived from singing are:

- acquiring language skills
- increasing vocabulary
- developing listening skills
- increasing attention span
- acquiring knowledge

- developing memory skills
- stimulating creativity
- learning to follow directions
- enhancing self-esteem
- releasing tension and reducing anxieties

It is easier to learn songs using both the visual and auditory senses. *Songs for the Flannel Board* offers new songs sung to familiar tunes with visual aids. The illustrations are to be prepared for the flannel board or a magnetic board. Activity ideas are included with each song for added reinforcement and enjoyment.

There are six sections in this book. *Humorous Songs* can help relieve stress and anxieties. The *Action Songs* enable children to get their "wiggles" out. *Colors* and *Dinosaurs* are among the most popular themes of pre-school and kindergarten teachers. The *Story Song* is a well-loved nursery tale written in lyric form to a favorite melody. *Quiet Time* helps children to relax.

Many of the songs encourage the children to express themselves through action and gesture which is an important part of language and communications. Children enjoy using motions to express the meaning of words and phrases. These actions help them retain what they have learned.

In several of the songs, the teacher is encouraged to write simple lyrics with the children. Children can express themselves freely, rhyming words if they are able. Some may choose to illustrate their original ideas. Creativity is always encouraged and praised.

One important word of advice: Do not be anxious if some children do not sing with the group. Parents tell us that children who were not participating at school are singing at home.

The illustrations in *Songs for the Flannel Board* are delightful and appealing to adults and children. They have been drawn in a manner which makes them easy to cut out.
Some tips for the pictures:
- Color brightly; children enjoy vivid colors.
- Protect with laminating film or contact paper; they will last longer.
- Attach pellon, sandpaper or felt tape on the back of each piece for use on the flannel board.
- Attach magnetic tape on the back of each piece for use on the magnetic board.
- Store in a large envelope, plastic bag, or manila folder; include the song with the pieces.

The activity ideas following the songs offer a wide variety of choices. There are suggestions for art, science, dramatic play, cooking, dramatization, movement, and many others. Teachers should adapt the activities to the appropriate age level of their class. Hopefully, these ideas will inspire many other fun-filled experiences.

The most important thing in using *Songs for the Flannel Board* is to have fun. Have fun singing the songs, changing the words, adding new verses, using the illustrations and doing the activities. Your enjoyment is contagious. Children will respond to your enthusiasm.

CONTENTS

Humorous Songs

A Silly Song 5

Song Pieces 6

The Bear (and others) Went Over The Mountain 9

Song Pieces 10

Color Songs

Party Hats 14

Song Pieces 15

Make A Rainbow 17

Song Pieces 19

Dinosaur Songs

Dinosaurs 21

Song Pieces 23

Pterosaurs 26

Song Pieces 27

Fossils 28

Song Pieces 30

Action Songs

A Walking We Will Go 34

Song Pieces 35

Here Comes the Rabbit Family 37

Song Pieces 39

Story Song

The Three Bears 42

Song Pieces 43

Quiet Time

Come Little Children 46

Song Pieces 47

Appendix

Music for *Songs for the Flannel Board* 49

A Silly Song

(Melody: "Have You Ever Seen A Lassie")

Have you ever met an **elephant**   *(put up elephant)*
An elephant, an elephant
Have you ever met an elephant
Who likes wearing clothes?   *(point to picture)*

Have you ever met a **dolphin**   *(put up dolphin)*
A dolphin, a dolphin
Have you ever met a dolphin
Who likes driving boats?   *(point to picture)*

Have you ever met a **gorilla**   *(put up gorilla)*
A gorilla, a gorilla
Have you ever met a gorilla
Who likes reading books?   *(point to picture)*

Have you ever met an **aardvark**   *(put up aardvark)*
An aardvark, an aardvark
Have you ever met an aardvark
Who likes eating ice cream?   *(point to picture)*

Have you ever met an **octopus**   *(put up octopus)*
An octopus, an octopus
Have you ever met an octopus
Who likes taking baths?   *(point to picture)*

Additional Activity Ideas

1. *Creative Thinking:* Have children name an animal they would like to meet and imagine the animal doing something funny or unusual. Sing their suggestions. This activity is especially good for the younger child. It is unrhymed.

2. *Art:* Invite children to illustrate an animal involved in a silly activity.

3. *Pantomine:* Have the children imitate the actions of the animals in the song. At the next session, the teacher should demonstrate each action. The children can guess which picture the teacher is demonstrating.

4. *Movement:* The children can copy the teacher in demonstrating the actions of the animals. Continue with other actions and body movements for the children to copy such as: scratching your head, blinking your eyes, shrugging your shoulders, bending your knees, and twisting your neck. Invite children to take turns being the leader.

(Elephant)

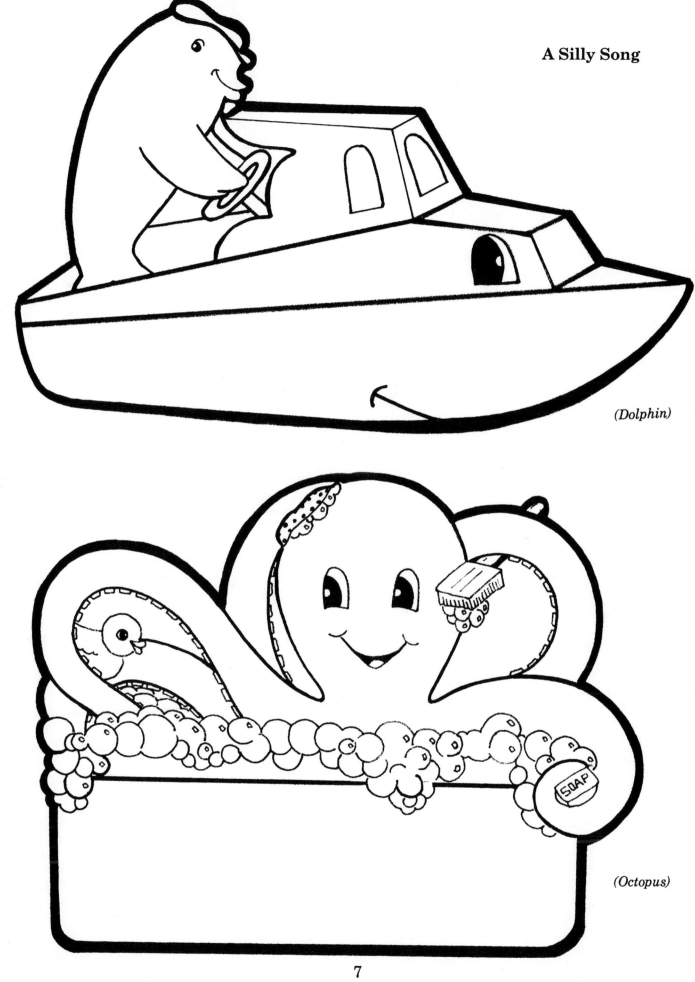

A Silly Song

(Dolphin)

(Octopus)

7

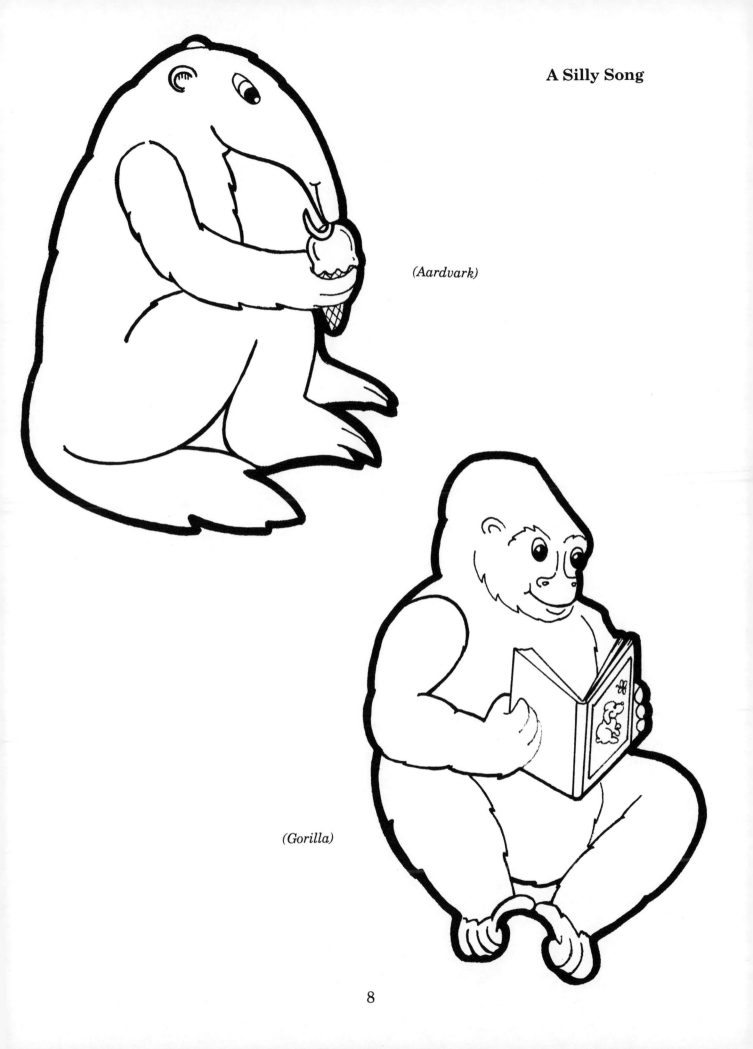

(Aardvark)

(Gorilla)

The Bear (and others) Went Over The Mountain

(Melody: "The Bear Went Over The Mountain")

The **bear** went over the mountain   *(put up bear)*
The bear went over the mountain
The bear went over the mountain
To see what he could see.
And all that he could see; and all that he could see
Was a **goat in a boat** - a goat in a boat   *(put up goat in boat)*
A goat in a boat - was all that he could see!

The **turtle** went over the mountain   *(put up turtle)*
The turtle went over the mountain
The turtle went over the mountain
To see what he could see.
And all that he could see; and all that he could see
Was a **skunk in a trunk** - a skunk in a trunk   *(put up skunk in trunk)*
A skunk in a trunk - was all that he could see!

The **rabbit** went over the mountain   *(put up rabbit)*
The rabbit went over the mountain
The rabbit went over the mountain
To see what he could see.
And all that he could see; and all that he could see
Was a **snake in a cake** - a snake in a cake   *(put up snake in cake)*
A snake in a cake - was all that he could see!

The **fox** went over the mountain   *(put up fox)*
The fox went over the mountain
The fox went over the mountain
To see what he could see.
And all that he could see; and all that he could see
Was a **monkey on a donkey**-a monkey on a donkey   *(put up monkey on donkey)*
A monkey on a donkey- was all that he could see!

Additional Activity Ideas

1. *Language-* Sing additional verses using more positional words:
   The fox went *under* a bridge.   The cat went *up* the tree.
   The snake went *down* the hole.
2. *Movement:* Vary the Actions. Sing additional verses using different motions and
   movements.
   The fox *marched* up the hill.   The frog *jumped* into the pond.
   The monkey *climbed* up the tree.   The turtle *dived* into the lake.
   The seagull *flew* over the ocean.
3. *Listening Skills:* Instruct the children to move in various ways to specific objects such as: walk to the desk, hop to the climber, crawl to the door, etc. Let children take turns giving directions.

**The Bear (and others)
Went Over The Mountain**

(Fox)

(Bear)

10

(Snake in Cake)

(Rabbit)

(Goat in Boat)

(Skunk in Trunk)

(Turtle)

(Monkey on Donkey)

Party Hats

(Melody: "London Bridges")

Robin wants the **red** hat, red hat, red hat.   *(put up "R" panda)*
Robin wants the red hat.
She likes red.   *(place RED hat on the "R" panda)*

Orville wants the **orange** hat, orange hat, orange hat. *(put up "O" panda)*
Orville wants the orange hat.
He likes orange.   *(place ORANGE hat on the "O" panda)*

Yentyl wants the **yellow** hat, yellow hat, yellow hat.   *(put up "Y" panda)*
Yentyl wants the yellow hat.
She likes yellow.   *(place YELLOW hat on the "Y" panda)*

Gavin wants the **green** hat, green hat, green hat.   *(put up "G" panda)*
Gavin wants the green hat.
He likes green.   *(place GREEN hat on the "G" panda)*

Becky wants the **blue** hat, blue hat, blue hat.   *(put up "B" panda)*
Becky wants the blue hat.
She likes blue.   *(place BLUE hat on the "B" panda)*

Peter wants the **purple** hat, purple hat, purple hat.   *(put up "P" panda)*
Peter wants the purple hat.
He likes purple.   *(place PURPLE hat on the "P" panda)*

All the bears have party hats, party hats, party hats.
All the bears have party hats.
They like parties!!

Additional Activity Ideas

1. *Color Awareness:* Designate a special color for each session. Invite children to wear that color or bring something of that color to class. Use the designated color for the art project, the snack and the story.
2. *Cognitive:* Have the children take turns matching each shirt with the party hat of the same color.
3. *Cognitive:* Put up all the panda bears. Have children name the colors of the shirts. Remove one panda. The children can guess which color is missing. Repeat this activity using the party hats.
4. *Art:* Have each child color and design white or light colored durable paper. Make into simple party hats. (This is a good activity for all ages. The design will be according to each individual's ability.)
5. *Art:* Offer copies of the panda bear pages to those children who enjoy coloring.

(Green Hat)

Party Hats

(Gavin)

(Red Hat)

(Orange Hat)

(Orville)

(Robin)

15

(Blue Hat)

Party Hats

(Becky)

(Purple Hat)

(Yellow Hat)

(Peter)

(Yentyl)

16

Make A Rainbow

(Melody: "Skip to My Lou")

(Put Rainbow Elf and pot on board)

Take some **cherries**; put them in a pot   *(put the cherries above the pot)*
Stir them, stir them, stir them a lot!
Pour it out now; what will it be?
The prettiest RED - you ever did see!!   *(put red strip at the top)*

Take an **orange**; put it in a pot   *(put the orange above the pot)*
Stir it, stir it, stir it a lot!
Pour it out now; what will it be?
The prettiest ORANGE - you ever did see!!   *(put orange strip under red strip)*

Take a **lemon**; put it in a pot   *(put the lemon above the pot)*
Stir it, stir it, stir it a lot!
Pour it out now; what will it be?
The prettiest YELLOW - you ever did see!!   *(put yellow strip under orange strip)*

Take some **limes** and put them in a pot   *(put the limes above the pot)*
Stir them, stir them, stir them a lot!
Pour it out now; what will it be?
The prettiest GREEN - you ever did see!!   *(put green strip under yellow strip)*

Take some **berries**; put them in a pot   *(put the blueberries above the pot)*
Stir them, stir them, stir them a lot!
Pour it out now; what will it be?
The prettiest BLUE - you ever did see!!   *(put blue strip under green strip)*

Take some **grapes** and put them in a pot   *(put the grapes above the pot)*
Stir them, stir them, stir them a lot!
Pour it out now; what will it be?
The prettiest PURPLE - you ever did see!!   *(put purple strip under blue strip)*

Red and orange, yellow and green-   *(point to each color as it is being sung)*
Blue and purple colors are seen!
Put them together; what will it be?   *(sweep hand across rainbow)*
The prettiest **rainbow** you ever did see!!

17

Additional Activity Ideas

1. *Cognitive:* Review the colors of the rainbow from top to bottom. (The last verse in the song lists the colors in order). Remove one color. Ask children to name the missing color.

2. *Art:* Offer children various media with which to make rainbows: crayons, markers, chalk, poster paint, finger paint, colored paper and paste.

3. *Group Project:* Draw the outline of a rainbow on a large sheet of paper. Within each section, paste the correct color. Invite the children to tear construction paper and continue to paste and fill in the sections. Variation: paste crushed squares of colored tissue paper for a dimensional effect.

4. *Nutritious Snack:* Make a rainbow fruit salad with strawberries, oranges, pineapple, green grapes, blueberries and purple grapes.

5. *Science:* Hang a prism in a sunny window. A prism will separate the white light passing through it into the colors of the rainbow.

(Red Cherries)

Make A Rainbow

(Gray Pot)

(Rainbow Elf)

(Purple Grapes)

19

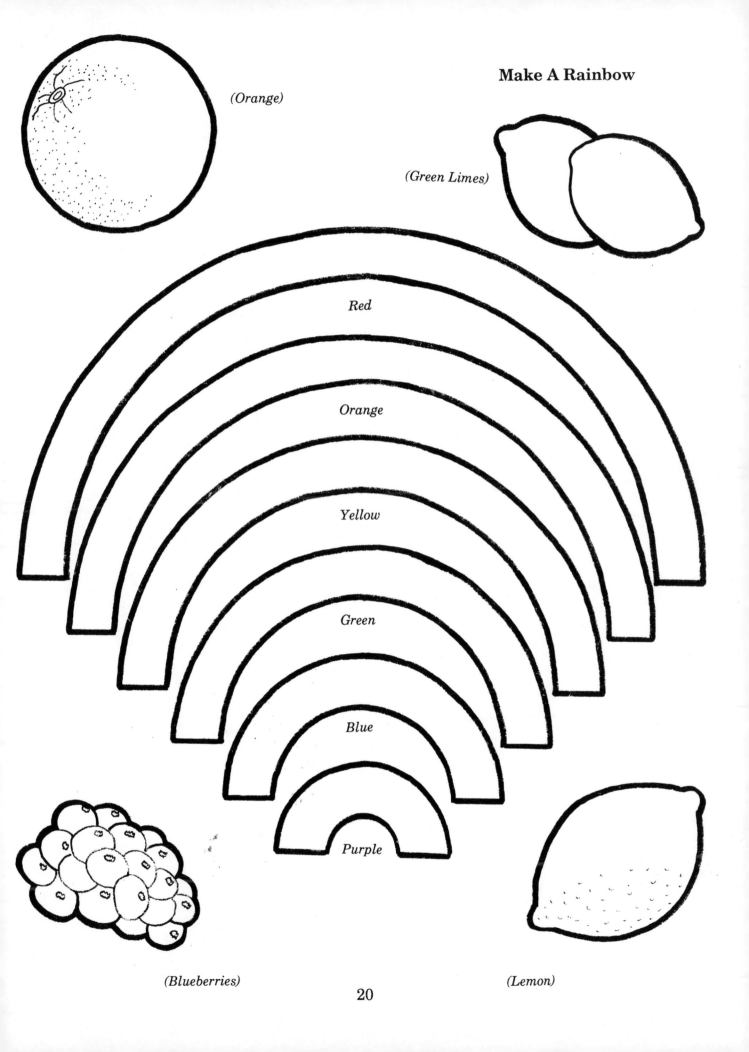

(Orange)

Make A Rainbow

(Green Limes)

Red

Orange

Yellow

Green

Blue

Purple

(Blueberries)

(Lemon)

20

Dinosaurs

Tyrannosaurus *(tie-ran-uh-SAWR-us)*
(Melody: "Battle Hymn of the Republic")

(put up Tyrannosaurus)

Tyrannosaurus is the King of all the dinosaurs
He's so strong and he's so mean and he gives loud and mighty roars
He is fierce and he is hungry and he has so many teeth
He looks for meat to eat.

Chorus:
Tyrannosaurus is a-coming
All the dinosaurs are running
Running from Tyrannosaurus
The King of Dinosaurs

Fact: Tyrannosaurus was the largest meat-eating dinosaur that ever lived.

Apatosaurus *(uh-PAT-uh-sawr-us)**
(Melody: "Yankee Doodle")

(put up Apatosaurus)

Apatosaurus is so big; he's very big and heavy
He stomps around to look for plants   *(put up palm tree)*
'Cause he is always hungry.

Apatosaurus eats all day; he's so very hungry
He eats all the plants he sees and that's what makes him happy.

Fact: Apatosaurus had a small mouth. It had to eat plants continuously to fill up it's big body.

*Note: Brontosaurus is the common, popular name for this large and heavy plant-eater. Nation-wide efforts are being made to use its correct scientific name, Apatosaurus, which was given by its first discoverer. Both names fit into the melody of this tune.

Triceratops (*try-SAIR-uh-tops*)

(Melody: "Three Blind Mice")

(put up Triceratops)

Look and see; one, two, three   *(point to each horn)*
Count with me; one two three   *(point to each horn)*
Triceratops has three big horns.   *(show three fingers)*
That's the way that he was born
One, two three; one two three!   *(again, point and count)*

Fact: Triceratops used its three, sharp horns for protection. He was very brave. While other dinosaurs would run, Triceratops would stay and fight Tyrannosaurus.

Additional Activity Ideas

1. *Art:* Make a positive stencil. Trace the outline of each of the three dinosaurs onto heavy paper or plastic (such as tagboard paper or plastic lids from large ice cream pails). Cut out the dinosaur. Child can trace around the stencil.

2. *Art:* Make a negative stencil. Trace outline of dinosaurs onto used X-Ray film. Cut and remove the traced figure. Tape the negative stencil onto sheet of newsprint paper. Invite child to paint within the cut-out figure. Remove X-Ray sheet to see painted dinosaur. Wash X-Ray film after each use.

3. *Movement:* Have children stomp around to the song, *Apatosaurus* and to the chorus of *Tyrannosaurus*.

(Tyrannosaurus)

(Apatosaurus)

Dinosaurs

(Palm Tree Plant)

(Tricertops)

25

Pterosaurs *(tair-uh-SAWRS)*

(extinct flying reptiles that lived in the time of the dinosaurs)

Pteranodon *(tair-AN-uh-don)*

(Melody: "The Farmer In The Dell")

Pteranodon can fly.   *(put up Pteranodon)*
He soars above the trees.
He spreads his giant wings   *(point to wings)*
And glides across the sea.

He opens up his beak;   *(point to beak)*
Inside there are no teeth.
He dives into the sea
And catches fish to eat.   *(point to fish)*

Fact: Pteranodon had a long toothless beak, a large crest at the back of the head and an enormous wing span that ranged from 20 to 27 feet.

Ramphorynchus *(RAM-for-rink-us)*

(Melody: "Twinkle, Twinkle Little Star")

Flying reptiles in the sky   *(put up Ramphorynchus)*
I would like to fly so high
Above the ocean I would soar
On my favorite pterosaur   *(point to Ramphorynchus)*
Ramphorynchus, spread your wings   *(sweep hand across wings)*
Let's go gliding while we sing!

Fact: Ramphorynchus had wings that spread about 4 feet. It had long, sharp teeth and a kite-like tail.

Additional Activity Ideas

1. *Art:* Make copies of the pterosaurs. Invite children to cut them out. Staple onto a straw. Children can move them so that the pterosaurs appear to be gliding.
2. *Cognitive:* Spend time discussing the differences between ramphorynchus and pteranodon. At the next session, ask questions about these two pterosaurs such as: Which one had teeth? Which one had a large bony crest on its head? Which had a long kite-like tail? Which one was bigger? Which one had wings as big as a child? Which one had wings as big as a telephone pole?
3. *Dramatization:* Have children pretend that they are pteranodons spreading their wings, soaring and gliding, diving into the sea, opening their beaks and catching fish to eat.
4. *Movement:* Have children pretend to be gliding as they sing, "Ramphorynchus".

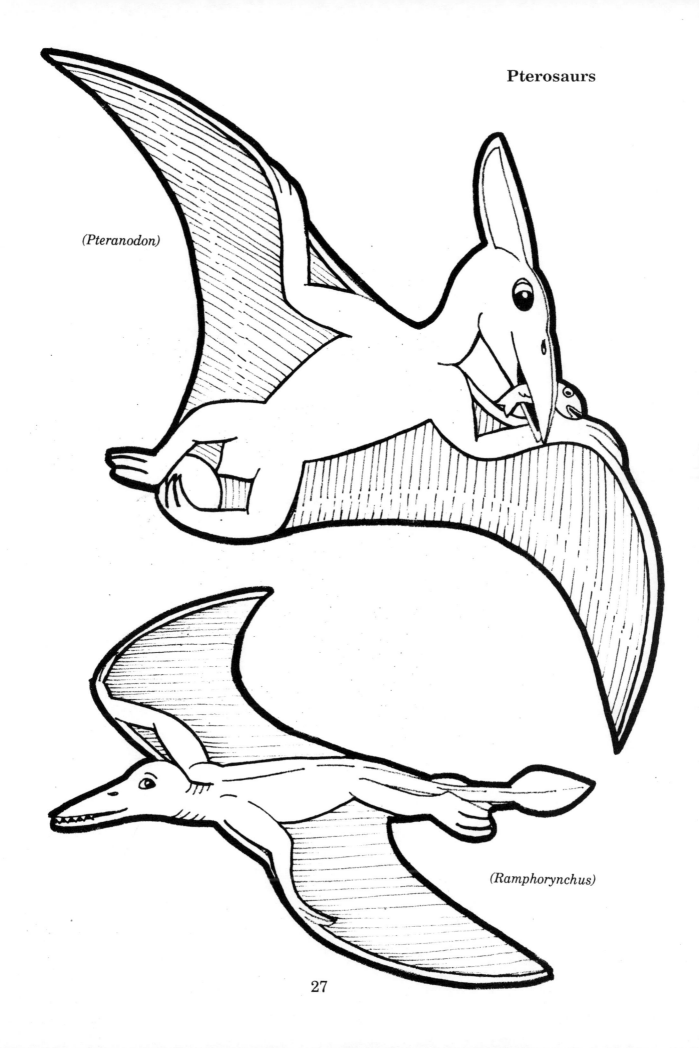

Pterosaurs

(Pteranodon)

(Ramphorynchus)

27

Fossils

All We Have Are Their Old Bones
(Melody: "My Darling Clementine")

Mighty dinosaurs - Flying pterosaurs   *(put up Tyrannosaurus and*
Lived so very long ago.   *Pteranodon)*
They are gone now - gone forever
All we have are their old bones!   *(put up bones of Tyrannosaurus*
                                                              and Pteranodon)

Long and tall bones - short and small bones   *(put up bones of Apatosaurus and*
They are buried in the ground.   *Ramphorynchus)*
Skeletons are put together -
From the bones that we have found.   *(put up bones of Triceratops)*

> *Fact:* Dinosaurs died out millions of years before people appeared on earth.
> We learn about them through discovery of their fossilized bones.

Those Bones
(Melody: "Dry Bones")

Those bones, those bones - from the dinosaurs   *(put up bones from Tyrannosaurus)*
Those bones, those bones - from the pterosaurs   *(put up bones from Pteradon)*
Those bones, those bones - from so long ago
They're buried deep in the ground.
We'll dig, we'll dig - we'll dig them up.

We'll dig, we'll dig - we'll dig them up.
We'll dig, we'll dig - we'll dig them up.
We'll dig them up from the ground.

We'll build, we'll build - a skeleton.   *(put up bones from Apatosaurus)*
We'll build, we'll build - a skeleton.
We'll build, we'll build - a skeleton.
From bones that came from the ground.

Those bones, those bones - from the dinosaurs   *(put up bones from Tricertops)*
Those bones, those bones - from the pterosaus   *(put up bones from Ramphoryncus)*
Those bones, those bones - from so long ago
I wish they could walk around!!

> *Fact:* Fossils are found almost everywhere and anyone can find them. They can be bones,
> shells, imprints of plants, insects, animal tracks.

Additional Activity Ideas

1. *Cognitive:* Have children match the drawings of the dinosaurs and pterosaurs with the drawings of their fossil bones; also match the plant with its fossil leaf.

2. *Dramatic Play:* Children can pretend to be scientists and dig up bones. The teacher can bury bones in a large pan of clean play sand for children to discover. (Teachers: Save large turkey bones. Boil to remove all meat. Rinse in water diluted with bleach. Rinse in clear water. Allow to dry well.)

3. *Science:* Have children study the "dinosaur" bones under a large magnifying glass. Bring in other fossils for them to study such as those found in rocks and shells. Go on a fossil hunt. (People who collect and study fossils are called paleontologists.)

4. *Math:* Make two piles of bones. Ask which pile has more bones. Have children count the bones.

5. *Dramatization:* Put actions to the verses of *Those Bones*. Stomp like a dinosaur, glide like a pterosaur, dig like a fossil hunter and build a skeleton like a Paleontalogist.

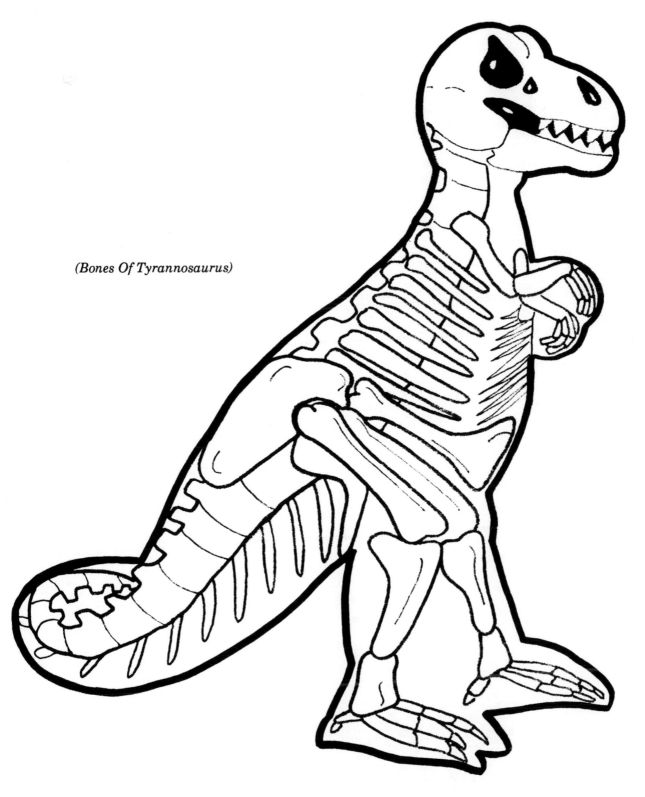

(Bones Of Tyrannosaurus)

(Bones Of Apatosaurus)

(Fossil Leaf)

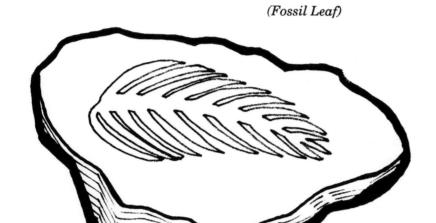

(Bones Of Tricertops)

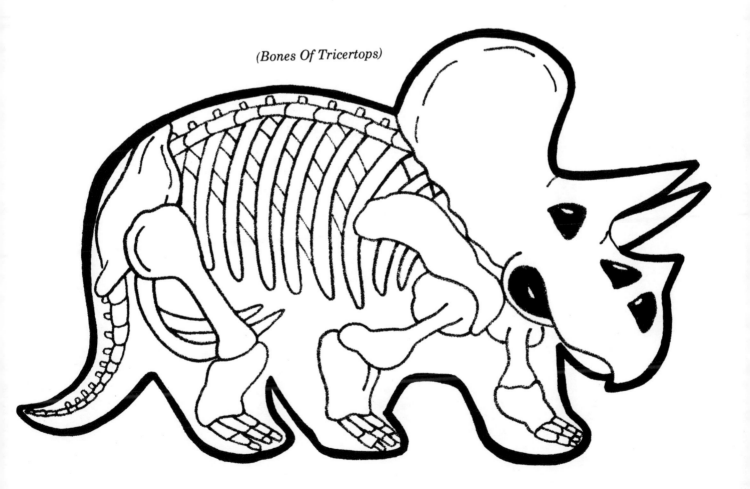

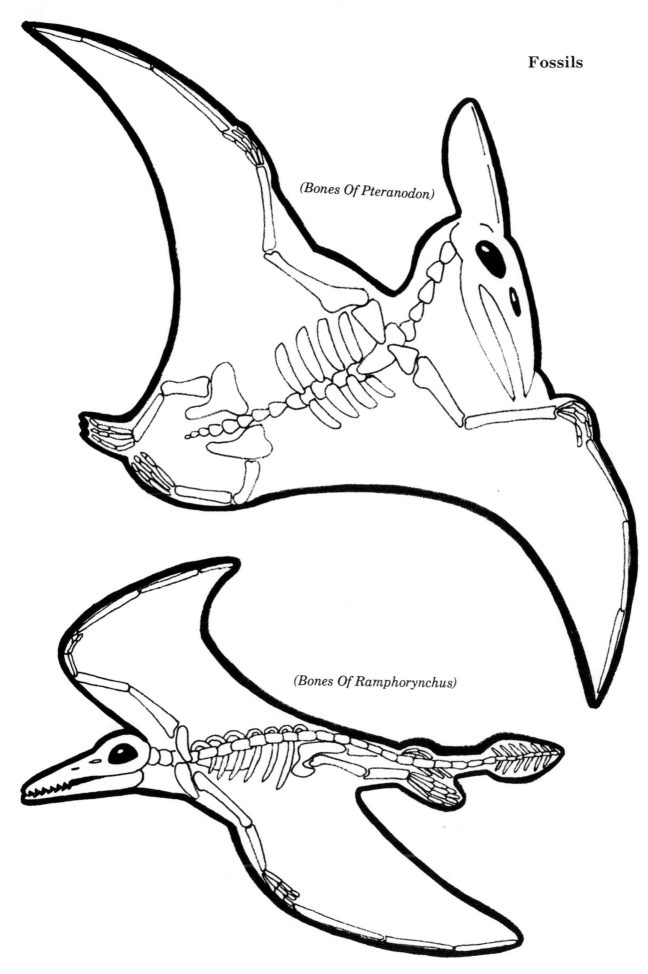

(Bones Of Pteranodon)

(Bones Of Ramphorynchus)

A-Walking We Will Go

(Melody: "A-Hunting We Will Go")

Oh, A-walking we will go; a-walking we will go
We'll see a **mouse building a house**   *(put up mouse/house)*
And say "It isn't so!"

Oh, A-walking we will go; a-walking we will go
We'll see a **duck driving a truck**   *(put up duck/truck)*
 And say "It isn't so!"

Oh, A-walking we will go; a-walking we will go
We'll see a **racoon up in a balloon**   *(put up racoon/balloon)*
And say "It isn't so!"

Oh, A-walking we will go; a-walking we will go
We'll see a **hog jogging with a frog**   *(put up hog/frog)*
And say "It isn't so!"

Oh, A-walking we will go; a-walking we will go
We'll see a **poodle dancing on a noodle**   *(put up poodle/noodle)*
And say "It isn't so!"

Additional Activity Ideas

1. *Movement:* Have the children walk "in place" as they sing. Have them stop and look at the picture on the flannel board while they sing the last two lines. Change the order of the pictures.
   a. Vary the Speed: walk (1) very slow (2) fast (3) normal
   b. Vary the Method: A-running we will go, a-skipping, a-hopping, a-jogging..
2. *Science:* Take a "Nature Walk" with the children. Instruct them to be very quiet and respectful of the animals and their habitat. Focus on using the senses. Instruct the children to look carefully, listen intently, and smell with eyes open and closed. Touching and tasting should be allowed only with supervision and approval of an adult.
3. *Language:* Have the class dictate a story about their nature walk.
4. *Listening Skills:* Instruct the children to move in various ways to specific objects such as: walk to the desk, hop to the climber, crawl to the door, etc. Let children take turns giving directions.

A-Walking We Will Go

(Mouse In House)

(Poodle On Noodle)

(Duck In Truck)

35

A-Walking We Will Go

(Racoon in Balloon)

(Hog and Frog)

36

The Rabbit Family Is Coming

(Melody: She'll Be Coming Round The Mountain")

(Put up Father Rabbit)

He'll be **flying in an airplane** when he comes - zoom, zoom!
He'll be flying in an airplane when he comes - zoom, zoom!
And we'll all go out to meet him; we'll be happy when we see him.
He'll be flying in an airplane when he comes - zoom, zoom!

(Put up Mother Rabbit)

She'll be **riding on a bicycle** when she comes - honk, honk!
She'll be riding on a bicycle when she comes - honk, honk!
And we'll all go out to meet her; we'll be happy when we see her.
She'll be riding on a bicycle when she comes - honk, honk!

(Put up Sister Rabbit)

She'll be **riding on a pony** when she comes - neigh, neigh!
She'll be riding on a pony when she comes - neigh, neigh!
And we'll all go out to meet her; we'll be happy when we see her.
She'll be riding on a pony when she comes - neigh. neigh!

(Put up Brother Rabbit)

He'll be **riding on a motorcycle** when he comes - vroom, vroom!
He'll be riding on a motorcycle when he comes - vroom, vroom!
And we'll all go out to meet him; we'll be happy when we see him.
He'll be riding on a motorcycle when he comes - vroom, vroom!

(Put up Baby Rabbit)

She'll be **riding in a wagon** when she comes - clickety, clack!
She'll be riding in a wagon when she comes - clickety, clack!
And we'll all go out to meet her; we'll be happy when we see her.
She'll be riding in a wagon when she comes - clickety, clack!

Additional Activity Ideas

1. *Language:* Ask children to suggest some other ways in which the Rabbit Family can come. Ideas: riding in a train, paddling a canoe, sailing in a boat, riding on a scooter, etc.
2. *Movement:* Have the children pretend to be flying, riding, galloping, pulling a wagon etc.
3. Instruments: Have the children play rhythm instruments to the beat of the song.
4. *Creative Thinking:* Ask the children "Where do you think the Rabbit Family is going?" Give them time to discuss different answers. Offer suggestions: to grandma's house, to visit an aunt or uncle, to the zoo, to the beach, to a park for a picnic etc.
5. *Lyric Writing:* Write your own verses; write verses with the children.

Additional Holiday Verses

Add the appropriate holiday verse to the end of the song.

Easter:

They'll be bringing chocolate bunnies when they come- Happy Easter!
They'll be bringing chocolate bunnies when they come- Happy Easter!
And we'll all go out to meet them; we'll be happy when we see them.
They'll be bringing chocolate bunnies when they come- Happy Easter!

Halloween:

They'll be wearing funny costumes when they come - Trick or Treat!
They'll be wearing funny costumes when they come - Trick or Treat!
And we'll all go out to meet them; we'll be happy when we see them.
They'll be wearing funny costumes when they come - Trick or Treat!

Thanksgiving:

And they'll bring a big fat turkey when they come - Yum, Yum!
And they'll bring a big fat turkey when they come - Yum, Yum!
And we'll all go out to meet them; we'll be happy when we see them.
And they'll bring a big fat turkey when they come - Yum, Yum!

Christmas:

And they'll bring a lot of presents when they come - Merry Christmas!
And they'll bring a lot of presents when they come - Merry Christmas!
And we'll all go out to meet them; we'll be happy when we see them.
And they'll bring a lot of presents when they come - Merry Christmas!

The Rabbit Family Is Coming

(Father Rabbit)

(Mother Rabbit)

39

(Sister Rabbit)

(Brother Rabbit)

(Baby Rabbit)

The Three Bears

(Melody: "The Ants Go Marching One By One")

Oh, here is Great Big **Papa Bear** - uh-huh, uh-huh   *(put up Papa Bear)*
And here is Medium-Size **Mama Bear** - uh-huh, uh-huh   *(put up Mama Bear)*
And here is little **Baby Bear**; he's the one with the fuzzy hair *(put up Baby Bear)*
And they all lived in the woods: deep in the woods
Deep in the woods - hmm, hmm, hmm.

Well, Papa Bear - he likes to build - uh-huh, uh-huh   *(put up saw)*
And Mama Bear - she likes to cook - uh-huh, uh-huh *(put up mixing bowl with spoon)*
And Baby Bear - he likes to play; he plays ball outside all day   *(put up ball/bat)*
And they all lived in the woods: deep in the woods
Deep in the woods - hmm, hmm, hmm.

A little girl named **Goldilocks** - uh-huh, uh-huh   *(put up Goldilocks)*
Went knocking on the three bears door - uh-huh, uh-huh   *(put up house)*
She walked into their house that day;
No one was there - they had gone a-way
They went walk-ing in the woods: deep in the woods
Deep in the woods - hmm, hmm, hmm.

The bears came back and found a mess, - uh-huh, uh-huh   *(put up chair/bowl)*
An empty bowl, a broken chair, - uh-huh, uh-huh   *(point to bowl; point to chair)*
They went upstairs to baby bear's bed
Goldilocks screamed and bumped her head!   *(put up Goldilocks in bed)*
And she ran a-way from the bears - deep in the woods
Deep in the woods, deep in the woods!   *(sung slower)*

Additional Activity Ideas

1. *Rhythm:* This song is excellent for clapping hands, slapping thighs, tapping chest, stomping feet, and striking rhythm instruments.

2. *Language:* Use the flannel board figures as stick puppets. Attach a small piece of the soft part of the velcro to the back of Goldilocks and each of the three bears. Glue a small piece of the rougher part of the velcro onto tongue depressor sticks. Attach the cut out characters onto the sticks by means of the velcro. Have four children hold up the appropriate character as the song is sung by the class.

3. *Dramatization:* Have children act out the parts of the four characters with the appropriate actions as the song is sung.

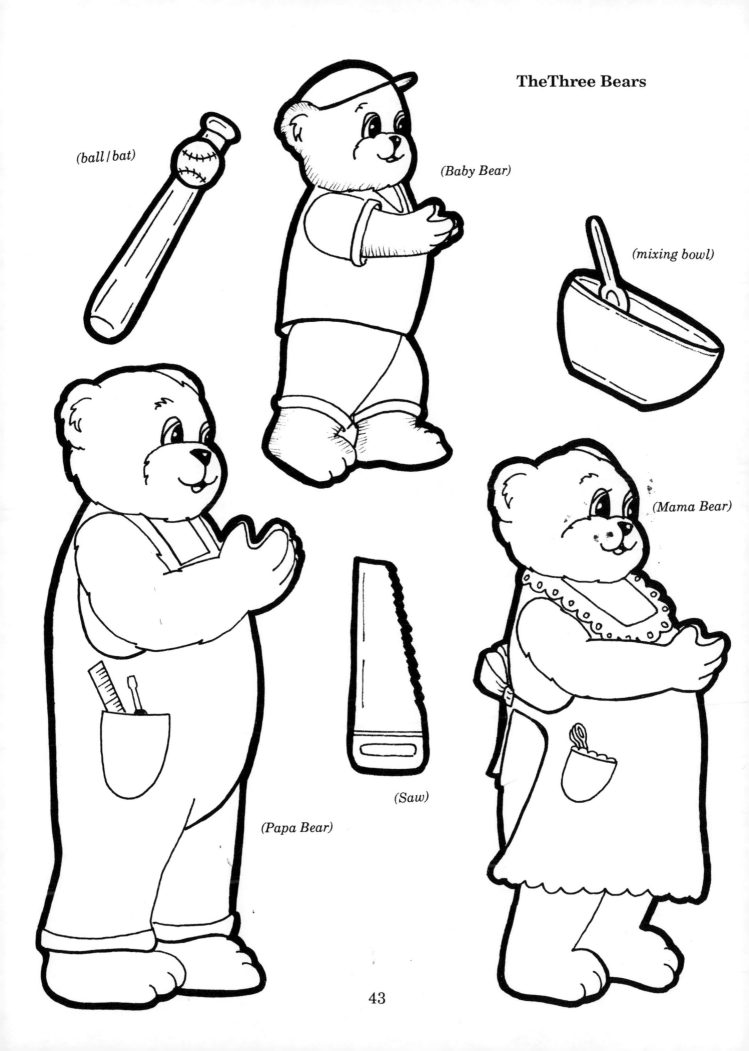

(ball / bat)

TheThree Bears

(Baby Bear)

(mixing bowl)

(Mama Bear)

(Papa Bear)

(Saw)

43

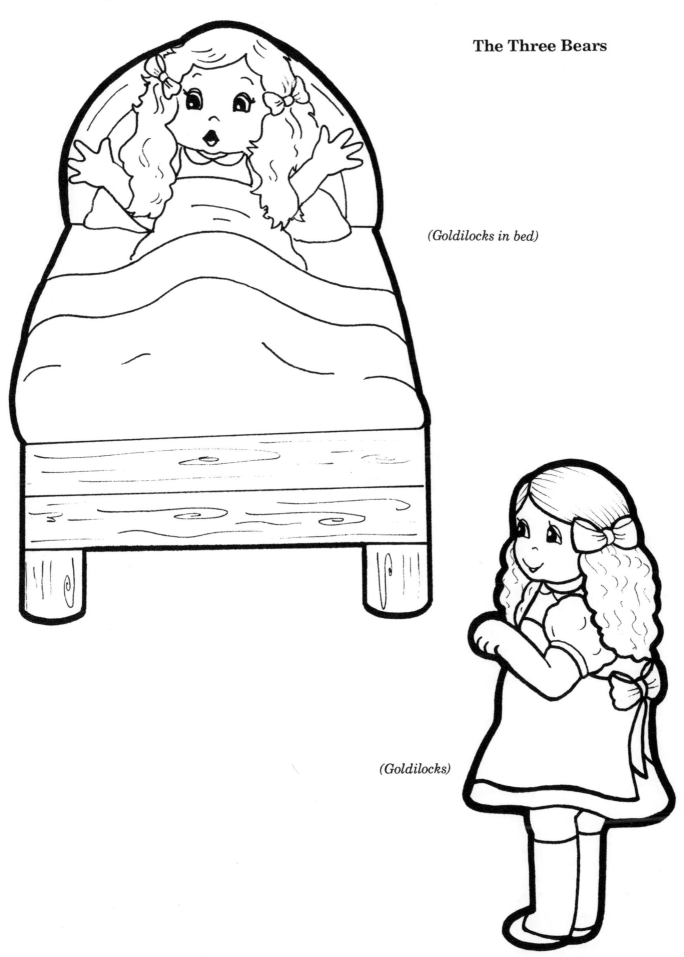

The Three Bears

(Goldilocks in bed)

(Goldilocks)

44

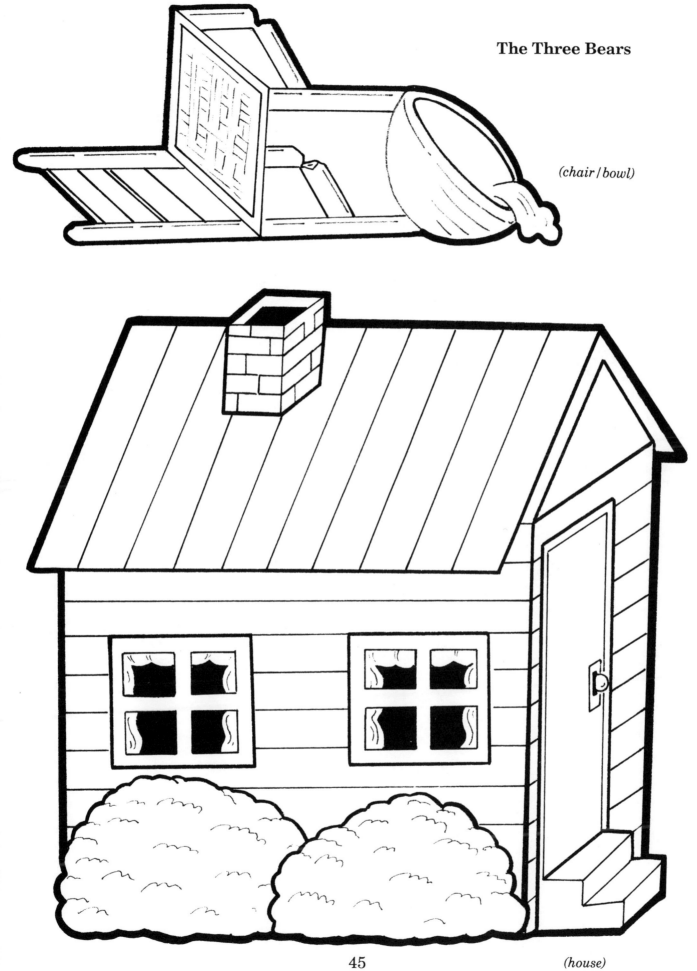

The Three Bears

(chair / bowl)

45

(house)

Come Little Children

(Melody: "Go Tell Aunt Rhody")

Refrain: Come little children; come little children
Come little children; it's time to go to sleep.

The **moon** is a'beaming; the moon is a'beaming;   *(put up moon)*
The moon is a'beaming; it's time to go to sleep.
The **stars** are a'shining; the stars are a'shining.   *(put up stars)*
The stars are a'shining; it's time to go to sleep.

Refrain: Come little children; come little children
Come little children; it's time to go to sleep.

The **puppies** are sleeping; the puppies are sleeping;   *(put up puppies)*
The puppies are sleeping; they do not make a peep.
The **kittens** are sleeping; the kittens are sleeping;   *(put up kittens)*
The kittens are sleeping; they do not make a peep.
The **bunnies** are sleeping; the bunnies are sleeping   *(put up bunnies)*
The bunnies are sleeping; they do not make a peep.

Refrain: Come little children; come little children
Come little children; it's time to go to sleep.

The **ponies** are sleeping; the ponies are sleeping;   *(put up ponies)*
The ponies are sleeping; they do not make a peep.
The **piglets** are sleeping; the piglets are sleeping;   *(put up piglets)*
The piglets are sleeping; they do not make a peep.
The **ducklings** are sleeping; the ducklings are sleeping;   *(put up ducklings)*
The ducklings are sleeping; they do not make a peep.

Refrain: Come little children; come little children
Come little children; it's time to go to sleep.

Additional Activity Ideas

1. *Relaxation:* Use this song to quiet the children. It has a calming effect.
2. *Movement:* Offer each child a scarf. Have them use the scarves to improvise expressive movement to the song.
3. *Language:* Invite children to name other baby farm animals such as lambs, chicks, goslings etc. Sing their suggestions.
4. *Science:* Talk about the farm animals in the song. Discuss where and how they sleep. Name woodland and jungle animals. Discuss their habitat and sleeping habits.
5. *Cognitive:* Collect pictures of various animals. Have children separate them into categories of where the animals live.

(Kittens)

(Bunnies)

(Puppies)

Come Little Children

(Piglets)

(Ducklings)

(Ponies)

48

MUSIC APPENDIX

A SILLY SONG
(Melody: "Have You Ever Seen A Lassie")

THE BEAR (and others) WENT OVER THE MOUNTAIN
(Melody: "The Bear Went Over The Mountain")

PARTY HATS
(Melody: "London Bridges")

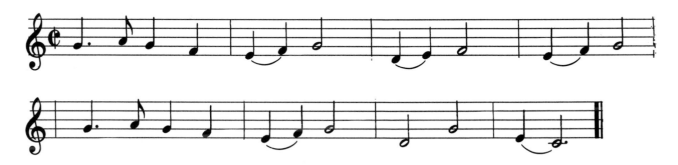

MAKE A RAINBOW
(Melody: "Skip To My Lou")

TYRANNOSAURUS
(Melody: "Battle Hymn Of The Republic")

APATOSAURUS
(Melody: "Yankee Doodle")

TRICERATOPS
(Melody: "Three Blind Mice")

PTERANODON
(Melody: "The Farmer In The Dell")

RAMPHORYNCHUS
(Melody: "Twinkle, Twinkle Little Star")

ALL WE HAVE ARE THEIR OLD BONES
(Melody: "My Darling Clementine")

THOSE BONES
(Melody: Dry Bones")

A WALKING WE WILL GO
(Melody: A Hunting We Will Go")

HERE COMES THE RABBIT FAMILY
(Melody: "She'll Be Coming Round The Mountain")

COME LITTLE CHILDREN
(Melody: "Go Tell Aunt Rhody")

THE THREE BEARS
(Melody: "The Ants Go Marching")